We Read
PHONICS™

I Want to Be a Cowboy!

TREASURE BAY

Parent's Introduction

Welcome to **We Read Phonics**! This series is designed to help you assist your child in reading. Each book includes a story, as well as some simple word games to play with your child. The games focus on the phonics skills and sight words your child will use in reading the story.

Here are some recommendations for using this book with your child:

1 Word Play

There are word games both before and after the story. Make these games fun and playful. If your child becomes bored or frustrated, play a different game or take a break.

I made the word book!

Now, can you change a letter to make the word cook?

Many of the games require printed materials (for example, sight word cards). You can print free game materials from your computer by going online to **www.WeReadPhonics.com** and clicking on the Game Materials link for this title. However, game materials can also be easily made with paper and a marker—and making them with your child can be a great learning activity.

② Read the Story

After some word play, read the story aloud to your child—or read the story together, by reading aloud at the same time or by taking turns. As you and your child read, move your finger under the words.

Next, have your child read the entire story to you while you follow along with your finger under the words. If there is some difficulty with a word, either help your child to sound it out or wait about five seconds and then say the word.

③ Discuss and Read Again

After reading the story, talk about it with your child. Ask questions like, "What happened in the story?" and "What was the best part?" It will be helpful for your child to read this story to you several times. Another great way for your child to practice is by reading the book to a younger sibling, a pet, or even a stuffed animal!

In the story, Roy wanted to be a cowboy. What would you like to be?

Either an astronaut or a racecar driver!

LEVEL 7 Level 7 introduces words with vowel combinations "ou" and "ow" (as in *out* and *owl*), "oi" and "oy" (as in *oil* and *boy*), "aw" (as in *hawk*), "oo" (as in *book*), and "oo" (as in *cool*).

I Want to Be a Cowboy!

A We Read Phonics™ Book
Level 7

Text Copyright © 2012 Treasure Bay, Inc.
Illustrations Copyright © 2012 Tim Raglin

Reading Consultants: Bruce Johnson, M.Ed., and Dorothy Taguchi, Ph.D.

We Read Phonics™ is a trademark of Treasure Bay, Inc.

Published by
Treasure Bay, Inc.
P.O. Box 119
Novato, CA 94948 USA

Printed in Malaysia

Library of Congress Catalog Card Number: 2011942420

Hardcover ISBN: 978-1-60115-351-7
Paperback ISBN: 978-1-60115-352-4
PDF E-Book ISBN: 978-1-60115-596-2

We Read Phonics™
Patent Pending

Visit us online at:
www.TreasureBayBooks.com

PR-6-12

I Want to Be a Cowboy!

By Sindy McKay

Illustrated by Tim Raglin

Making Words

Creating words with these letter combinations will help your child read the words in this story.

Materials:

Option 1—Fast and Easy: To print free game materials from your computer, go online to www.WeReadPhonics.com, then go to this book title and click on the link to "View & Print: Game Materials."

Option 2—Make Your Own: You'll need thick paper or cardboard, crayon or marker, and scissors. Cut fifteen 2 x 2 inch squares from the paper or cardboard and print these letters and letter combinations on the squares: ou, ow, aw, oo, a, b, t, m, n, f, d, s, l, c, r, and k.

1 Place the cards letter side up in front of your child.

2 Ask your child to make and say words using the letters available. For example, your child could choose the letters "l," "ou," and "d," and make the word *loud*.

3 If your child has difficulty, try presenting letters that will make a specific word. For example, present "b," "oo," and "k", and ask your child to make *book*. You could then ask your child to find a letter to change the word to *look*.

4 Ask your child to make as many words as possible that use the "ou," "ow," "aw," and "oo" cards. These letter patterns are used in the story. Possible words include *out, about, mount, found, sound, loud, cow, now, owl, books, brook, broom, look, soon, moon, stool* and *boots*.

Sight Word Game

Word Cubes

This is a fun way to practice some sight words used in the story.

Materials:

Option 1 – Fast and Easy: To print free game materials from your computer, go online to www.WeReadPhonics.com, then go to this book title and click on the link to "View & Print: Game Materials."

Option 2 – Make Your Own: You'll need paper or thin cardboard, pencil, scissors, and tape. Using the pattern on the right, make two cube outlines on a separate piece of paper or thin cardboard. Before cutting out or folding, write each of the following 12 words on one face of each of the two cube outlines:

about, once, around, outside, want, said, they, could, very, one, little, good

Cut out the cube outlines. Fold on the dotted lines. Tape the flaps to make the two cubes.

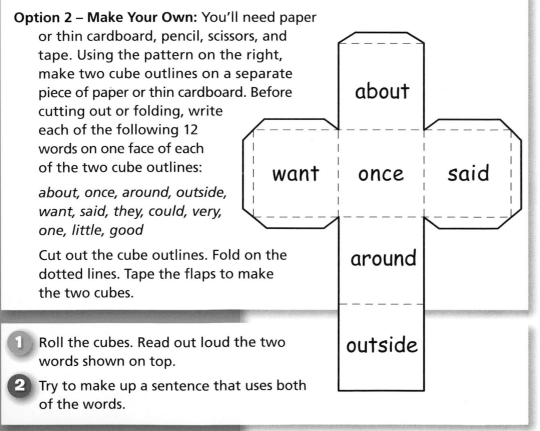

1 Roll the cubes. Read out loud the two words shown on top.

2 Try to make up a sentence that uses both of the words.

3

Roy Brown wanted to be a cowboy. He had books about cowboys. He had a cowboy hat and boots. But Roy had never seen a real cow.

So Roy went to a dude ranch. Here he could ride a pony and sleep outside. He could see a real cow!

Roy showed up at noon. A man named Hawk met him at the gate. Roy said to Hawk, "I want to be a cowboy!"

Hawk spoke with a Texas drawl.
"It takes more than a hat and boots
to be a cowboy."

Roy scowled. "I will make a good cowboy. Look!" Roy found a broom and said, "Pretend this is a cow. I will rope it."

8

The rope did not go around the broom.
Then Roy saw a bale of straw. "Pretend it
is a pony," he said. "I will mount it."

Roy ran to jump on the pony. He missed.
Hawk asked Roy, "Can you milk a cow?"
"Yes," said Roy.

Roy sat on a stool and did his best. It did not go well.

Hawk told Roy not to feel too bad.
"Soon we will take the herd out on the
trail," he said. "You will have fun."

The next day they set out. Roy pouted. "Maybe I do not want to be a cowboy after all."

Then Roy stopped. He could hear a
sound. It was like a baby bawling.

The sound was a baby cow! Roy found
her in a brook. She could not get out.

Roy yelled for help. He was very loud, but no one could hear him.

The little cow was loud too!
How could Roy get her out of the brook?

Roy saw this once in a cowboy book.
The cowboy put a rope on the cow. Then
he led her out.

"That is what I will do," Roy said to his pony. He took out his coiled rope and twirled it.

"Now we will lead her out," said Roy.
The pony began to go, and the little
cow came out.

Roy was proud. Then he looked up. He saw Hawk!

"Good work," said Hawk. "Now you can take her back to the herd."

Roy led the way. He took the little cow
to her mother.

That night there was a big moon in the sky. Roy could hear the hoot of an owl. Roy felt good.

Hawk spoke to the cowboys around
the fire. "Roy did a good thing today," he
said. "He rescued a little cow."

Hawk put his hat on Roy and said,
"Now you are a real cowboy."

Phonics Game

Word Cross

Creating words from these letters will help your child practice building words like those in this story.

Materials:

Option 1— Fast and Easy: To print free game materials from your computer, go online to www.WeReadPhonics.com, then go to this book title and click on the link to "View & Print: Game Materials."

Option 2—Make Your Own: Use the same letter cards created for Making Words (see page 2). Consider adding another two letter cards each for "a," "o," "u," and "w."

1 Place the cards with the letter side down on a table. Each player draws five cards.

2 The first player tries to make a word using the cards. If no word can be made, the player discards one card and draws another card, and it becomes the next player's turn.

3 If the first player can make a word using the cards, the player makes the word going across. After making a word, a player receives one point for each letter used and draws enough cards to maintain five cards.

4 Subsequent words must be built upon words previously made, either across or down, in a crossword pattern. For example, if the first player builds the word *sound,* then the next player must build a word going down, using "s," "ou," "n," or "d," such as *stool* or *town.*

5 Consider playing with both players showing their letters and helping each other.

Guess the Word

This is a fun way to practice blending letter sounds together, which helps children learn to read new words.

c...ow...b...oy

Cowboy!

1 Choose a simple word in the story that can be sounded out. Say the sound for each letter or letter combination in the word. For example, for the word *cowboy,* say the sounds for the letters "c," "ow" (as in *cow*), "b," and "oy" (as in *boy*), with a slight pause between the sounds.

2 Ask your child to guess or say the word.

3 If your child does not reply correctly, then repeat and extend the sounds. If your child continues to have difficulty, run the sounds closer and closer together.

4 Continue with additional words from the story, such as *outside, pouted, found, around, brown, scowled, hawk, bawling, books, brook, hoot,* and *noon.*

5 For variation, let your child provide the prompt sounds to you.

If you liked *I Want to Be a Cowboy!*,
here is another **We Read Phonics** book you are sure to enjoy!

A Day at the Zoo

Just open this book for a trip to the zoo! There are lots of animals to see. At the zoo, you might see some scary reptiles, some odd birds, or some very strange insects. You might even get to feed and pet some of the animals!